Diwali

Holidays around the world

Jessica Coupé

LIGHTBOX
openlightbox.com

LIGHTBOX

Go to
www.openlightbox.com
and enter this book's
unique code.

ACCESS CODE

LBXZ6782

Lightbox is an all-inclusive digital solution for the teaching and learning of curriculum topics in an original, groundbreaking way. Lightbox is based on National Curriculum Standards.

OPTIMIZED FOR

- ✓ TABLETS
- ✓ SMART BOARDS
- ✓ COMPUTERS
- ✓ AND MUCH MORE!

STANDARD FEATURES OF LIGHTBOX

- **AUDIO** High-quality narration using text-to-speech system
- **VIDEOS** Embedded high-definition video clips
- **ACTIVITIES** Printable PDFs that can be emailed and graded
- **WEBLINKS** Curated links to external, child-safe resources
- **SLIDESHOWS** Pictorial overviews of key concepts
- **INTERACTIVE MAPS** Interactive maps and aerial satellite imagery
- **QUIZZES** Ten multiple choice questions that are automatically graded and emailed for teacher assessment
- **KEY WORDS** Matching key concepts to their definitions

SUPPLEMENTARY RESOURCES

- **SHARE** Share titles within your Learning Management System (LMS) or Library Circulation System
- **CURRICULUM** Find national and state curriculum correlations
- **CITATION** Create bibliographical references following APA, CMSO, and MLA styles

VIDEOS

WEBLINKS

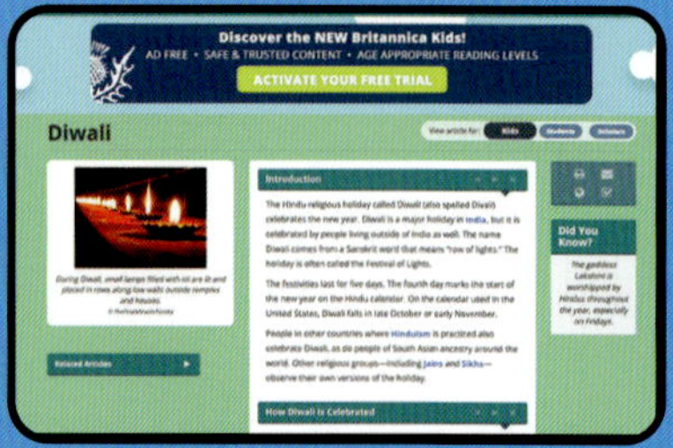

SLIDESHOWS

QUIZZES

This title is part of our Lightbox digital subscription

Lightbox Grades K–2 Subscription
ISBN 978-1-5105-5423-8

Access hundreds of Lightbox titles with our digital subscription.
Sign up for a **FREE** subscription trial at **www.openlightbox.com/trial**

The digital components of this book are guaranteed to stay active for at least five years from the date of publication.

Holidays around the world

Diwali

CONTENTS

Diwali is a Hindu festival celebrated in October or November each year. It lasts for five days.

Diwali is often called the "Festival of Lights."

6

Diwali celebrates the victory of light over darkness and good over evil.

It began as a Hindu religious holiday. Today, it is also important in the Sikh and Jain faiths.

People decorate their homes with *diyas*, or oil lamps. They may also light candles and put up colorful electronic lights.

The city of Ayodhya, in India, burns more than 1.5 million diyas during Diwali.

The largest Diwali festivities are held in India and other countries in South Asia.

Celebrations also take place in the United States and around the world.

Diwali has been celebrated in **India** for more than **2,500 years.**

Families and friends often gather for a large meal.

Traditional Indian snacks, such as ladoos and samosas, are popular during Diwali.

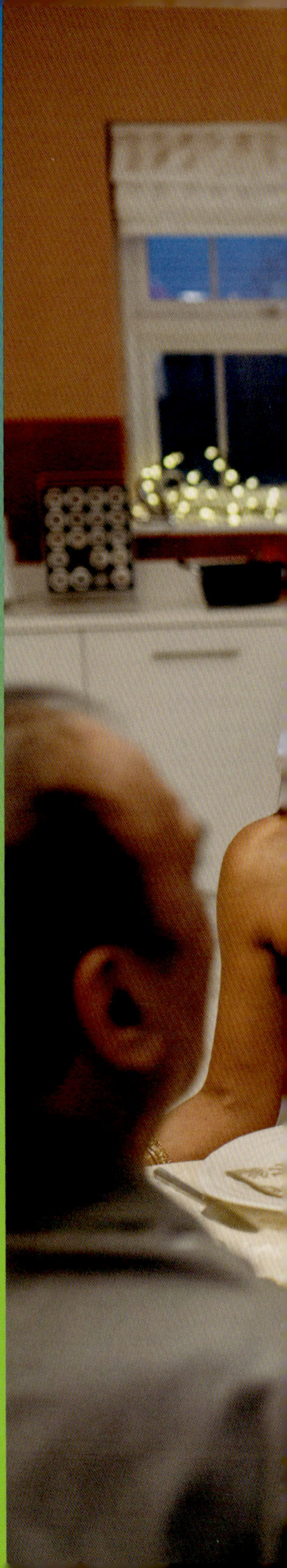

14

Colorful designs called rangolis are drawn on the ground. They are often circular and can be made of colored powder.

The world's **largest rangoli** covered an area of more than **420,000 square feet** (39,000 square meters).

People clean their homes during Diwali. They draw rangolis to invite the Hindu goddess Lakshmi to visit.

Lakshmi is the goddess of wealth and prosperity.

People donate money, food, toys, and other gifts during Diwali.

It is a time to spread joy and help those in need.

Firecrackers are a large part of Diwali celebrations. Children and adults often hold sparklers.

Fountains and rockets are lit up in public displays.

DIWALI FACTS

These pages provide more detail about the interesting facts found in the book. They are intended to be used by adults as a learning support to help young readers round out their knowledge of each holiday featured in the *Holidays around the World* series.

Pages 4–5

Diwali is a Hindu festival celebrated in October or November. It likely began as a harvest festival. Diwali's exact date varies according to the Hindu lunar calendar. It is observed over a five-day period in the Hindu month of Kartik. The main celebration is held on the third day.

Pages 6–7

Diwali celebrates the victory of light over darkness and good over evil. It is an important festival not only for Hindus but also for Sikhs and Jains. According to one of the legends associated with Diwali, Prince Rama, an incarnation of the Hindu god Vishnu, embarked on a heroic quest to rescue his wife Sita, an incarnation of the Hindu goddess Lakshmi, from the demon king Ravana. Upon their triumphant return, they saw the city of Ayodhya glowing with lights to welcome them back.

Pages 8–9

People decorate their homes with *diyas*, or oil lamps. Diyas have a circular base and a spout, as well as a cotton wick soaked in oil. According to Hindu tradition, 13 diyas should be lit during Diwali. Each has a special meaning. Diwali gets its name from the Sanskrit word *Deepavali*, which means "row of lights." The holiday is sometimes called Deepavali, too.

Pages 10–11

The largest Diwali festivities are held in India and other countries in South Asia. Diwali is a national holiday in India and is marked by fireworks, decorations, lit diyas, and joyful gatherings. The celebration extends to neighboring countries such as Nepal, Sri Lanka, Malaysia, and Singapore. Events are also held among the South Asian diaspora in the United States and other Western countries.

Pages 12–13

Families and friends often gather for a large meal. People treat themselves to snacks and sweet desserts. Samosas are a common snack. They are made of deep-fried dough filled with mashed potato, peas, and spices. Many different sweets are exchanged as gifts during Diwali. Ladoos, which are spherical desserts made of flour and sugar, are a popular choice.

Pages 14–15

Colorful designs called rangolis are drawn on the ground. Rangoli patterns are often inspired by nature. These temporary artworks can be made using many different mediums, including colored powders, rice, sand, or even flower petals. Circular designs are common, but rangolis can be shaped into animals, trees, flowers, and more.

Pages 16–17

People clean their homes and draw rangolis to invite the Hindu goddess Lakshmi to visit. A clean home is thought to attract positive energy. It prepares a welcoming environment for Lakshmi, making her more likely to visit. Since Lakshmi is the goddess of wealth and prosperity, her presence is believed to bring good fortune to a household.

Pages 18–19

Diwali is a time to spread joy and help those in need. People are encouraged to practice *dana*, or "charitable giving," and *seva*, or "selfless service." They may gift money to workers or toys to children in need. Some people donate food, blankets, and medical supplies to charities or directly to individuals.

Pages 20–21

Firecrackers are a big part of the Diwali celebrations. Sparklers called *fuljhari* are especially popular. These handheld sticks emit sparks when lit and create patterns of light as they are waved through the air. *Chakri* are spinning wheel fireworks. Fountains produce cascading showers of sparks, and rockets shoot high into the sky before exploding.

KEY WORDS

Research has shown that as much as 65 percent of all written material published in English is made up of 300 words. These 300 words cannot be taught using pictures or learned by sounding them out. They must be recognized by sight. This book contains 57 common sight words to help young readers improve their reading fluency and comprehension. This book also teaches young readers several important content words, such as proper nouns. These words are paired with pictures to aid in learning and improve understanding.

Page	Sight Words First Appearance
4	a, days, each, for, in, is, it, lasts, lights, of, often, or, the, year
7	also, and, as, began, good, important, over
8	city, homes, may, more, people, put, than, their, they, up, with
11	are, around, been, has, other, place, states, take, world
12	large, such
15	an, be, can, feet, made, on
16	to
19	food, help, need, those, time
20	children, part

Page	Content Words First Appearance
4	Diwali, festival, November, October
7	darkness, evil, faiths, holiday, victory
8	Ayodhya, candles, diyas, India, oil lamps
11	celebrations, countries, festivities, South Asia, United States
12	families, friends, ladoos, meal, samosas, snacks
15	area, designs, ground, powder, rangolis
16	goddess, Lakshmi, prosperity, wealth
19	gifts, joy, money, toys
20	adults, displays, firecrackers, fountains, rockets, sparklers

Published by Lightbox Learning Inc.
276 5th Avenue, Suite 704 #917
New York, NY 10001
Website: www.openlightbox.com

Library of Congress Cataloging-in-Publication Data

Names: Coupé, Jessica, author.
Title: Diwali / Jessica Coupé.
Description: New York, NY : Lightbox Learning Inc., [2024] | Series: Holidays around the world
Identifiers: LCCN 2023043866 (print) | LCCN 2023043867 (ebook) | ISBN 9781510567351 (library binding) | ISBN 9781510567368
Subjects: LCSH: Divali--Juvenile literature.
Classification: LCC BL1239.82.D58 C68 2024 (print) | LCC BL1239.82.D58 (ebook) | DDC 294.5/36--dc23/eng/20231023
LC record available at https://lccn.loc.gov/2023043866
LC ebook record available at https://lccn.loc.gov/2023043867

Printed in Guangzhou, China
1 2 3 4 5 6 7 8 9 0 27 26 25 24 23

102023
110822

Project Coordinator: Priyanka Das
Art Director: Terry Paulhus
Layout: Jean Faye Marie Rodriguez

The publisher acknowledges Alamy, Getty Images, and Shutterstock as the primary image suppliers for this title.